The Misanthrope

Molière (1622–73) was born Jean Poquelin, the son of a prosperous upholsterer of Paris. His father was attached to the service of the King and Molière was intended to succeed him. However, in 1643 he changed his surname and joined a family of actors, the Béjarts. Encouraged by their touring success the group returned to Paris and performed in front of Louis XIV and his Court. The success of Molière's farce *Le Docteur Amoureux* gave the group the opportunity to share a theatre at the Petit-Bourbon with an Italian company, and here Molière's reputation was established. His other plays include *L'Ecole des Femmes* (1662), *Don Juan* (1665), *Tartuffe* (written 1664, produced 1667), *Le Bourgeois Gentilhomme* (1671), *Les Femmes Savantes* (1673) and *Le Malade Imaginaire* (1673).

Martin Crimp was born in 1956. His plays include *Definitely the Bahamas* (1987), *Dealing with Clair* (1988), *Play with Repeats* (1989), *No One Sees the Video* (1990), *Getting Attention* (1991), *The Treatment* (winner of the 1993 John Whiting Award), *Attempts on Her Life* (1997), *The Country* (2000), *Face to the Wall* (2002), *Cruel and Tender* (2004), *Fewer Emergencies* (2005) and *The City* (2008). He has a longstanding relationship with London's Royal Court Theatre, and more recently with the Vienna Festival and the Festival d'Automne in Paris, which commissioned his first text for music, *Into the Little Hill* (2006), written for composer George Benjamin. He has also translated works by Ionesco, Koltès, Genet, Marivaux, Molière and Chekhov.

also by Martin Crimp

MARTIN CRIMP PLAYS ONE
(*Dealing with Clair, Play with Repeats,
Getting Attention, The Treatment*)

PLAYS TWO
(*No One Sees the Video, The Misanthrope,
Attempts on Her Life, The Country*)

THREE ATTEMPTED ACTS
(in *Best Radio Plays of 1985*)

FACE TO THE WALL *and* FEWER EMERGENCIES

CRUEL AND TENDER

THE CITY

Translations

THE CHAIRS (Ionesco)
RHINOCEROS (Ionesco)
THE MISANTHROPE (Molière)
ROBERTO ZUCCO (Koltès)
THE MAIDS (Genet)
THE TRIUMPH OF LOVE (Marivaux)
THE FALSE SERVANT (Marivaux)
THE SEAGULL (Chekhov)
PAINS OF YOUTH (Bruckner)

MOLIÈRE

The Misanthrope

in a version by
MARTIN CRIMP

faber and faber

First published 1996
This revised edition first published in 2009
by Faber and Faber Limited
74–77 Great Russell Street
London WC1B 3DA

Typeset by Country Setting, Kingsdown, Kent CT14 8ES
Printed in England by CPI Bookmarque, Croydon, Surrey

A CIP record for this book
is available from the British Library

ISBN 978–0–571–25951–9

2 4 6 8 10 9 7 5 3

Rewriting Molière

For all its formal brilliance, *Le Misanthrope* (1666) is
one of Molière's most intensely personal plays. The fierce
argument between conformity and nonconformity clearly
derives from his experience of the scandals surrounding
three plays of the early 1660s – *L'Ecole des Femmes, Le
Tartuffe* and *Dom Juan* – where the writer found himself
accused of obscenity, and, more dangerously, of atheism.
The voices of righteous anger (Alceste) on the one hand
and reasonable compromise (Philinte) on the other must
have been continually whispering inside his head like
good and bad angels as he struggled to come to terms
with the ambiguity of his position as both satirist and
servant of the cultural and political elite. And it's hard
not to see in the play's central relationship – etched in
acid – between a middle-aged man and a woman half his
age a reference to Molière's own personal life, after his
marriage in 1661, aged forty, to Armande Béjart, a
young actress of 'vingt ans ou environ'. Equally, it would
be a mistake to see Alceste as a self-portrait. The writer
remains detached from his character. This is why Alceste,
despite the serious overtones, remains a comic creation.
In the words of Francine Mallet, 'Alceste is Molière
without the irony. Molière knows he looks ridiculous in
some situations – Alceste doesn't.'

So how do you 'translate' (literally 'move from one place
to another') an artefact that is so much a product of
seventeenth-century Paris and Versailles? One answer –
and the one I've attempted here – is to opt for a contemporary setting, and then explore the consequences,

whatever deviations and departures from the original that may involve. Molière himself was adamant about the actuality of comedy: 'When you portray [tragic] heroes, you can do what you like. They're imaginary portraits, in which we don't expect to recognise ourselves . . . But when you portray real people, you have to paint what you see. The pictures must be accurate. If you don't make *recognisable portraits of the contemporary world*, then nothing's been achieved' (*La Critique de l'Ecole des Femmes*, Scene vi, italics mine). And if, three hundred years later, reflecting the contemporary world has meant taking certain 'liberties' with the text, this is only in the belief that – at this distance in time – reinvention, rewriting of one writer's work by another, is 'fidelity' of the truest and most passionate kind.

On 17 February 1673, Molière, whose health had been deteriorating for some time, coughed up blood during the final scene of *Le Malade Imaginaire*, at the point where the character he played was being 'initiated' as a doctor, in a scathing parody of the medical profession he so abhorred. After the performance he was carried in his chair back to his home in the rue de Richelieu. Two priests refused to come, and a third was too late: he died the same night, aged fifty-one.

His enemies weren't slow to savour the irony. One anonymous poem puts these words into his mouth:

> I performed character-assassinations
> with impunity on kings, the devout, marquis,
>   people of all stations.
> I found the hidden truth behind every character,
> but came to grief playing the part of doctor.
> I died without medical, spiritual or legal aid.
> I played death itself – and with death itself I paid.

A week after Molière's death, on 24 February, his theatre reopened with a production of *Le Misanthrope*.

Martin Crimp
November 1995

For background to Molière's life and work I am indebted to Francine Mallet's Molière (*Paris: Grasset, 1986*), *from which I have quoted above.*

The **Misanthrope** in this new version was first performed at the Young Vic, London, on 8 February 1996. The cast was as follows:

John William Osborne
Alceste Ken Stott
Covington Niall Buggy
Jennifer Elizabeth McGovern
Ellen Cathryn Bradshaw
Alexander Richard O'Callaghan
Julian Jo Stone-Fewings
Messenger/Simon George Beach
Marcia Linda Marlowe

Director Lindsay Posner
Designer Joanna Parker
Lighting Designer Simon Corder
Music Paddy Cunneen
Sound Designer John A. Leonard

The **Misanthrope** in this version was revived at the Comedy Theatre, London, on 7 December 2009, presented by Howard Panter and Tali Pelman for The Ambassador Theatre Group, Sweet Pea Productions and Tulchin/Bartner Productions. The cast was as follows:

Alceste Damian Lewis
Jennifer Keira Knightley
Marcia Tara FitzGerald
John Dominic Rowan
Covington Tim McMullen
Alexander Nicholas Le Prevost
Ellen Kelly Price
Julian Chuk Iwuji
Messenger/Simon James Hogg

Director Thea Sharrock
Designer Hildegard Bechtler
Costume Designer Amy Roberts
Lighting Designer Peter Mumford
Sound Designer Ian Dickinson

Notes

When a slash (/) appears within the text, this marks
the point of interruption in overlapping dialogue.

Character prefixes have been placed centrally
to conform to the printing practice of Molière's time.

The first syllable of Covington rhymes with 'love'.
Marcia rhymes with 'classier'.

Characters

Alceste
a playwright

John
his friend

Covington
a critic

Jennifer
a movie star

Ellen
a journalist

Marcia
a teacher of acting

Julian
an actor

Alexander
an agent

Also required
A Motorbike Messenger
Simon, a musician

All characters are British, except Jennifer,
who is an American.

The time is now, the place is London.

THE MISANTHROPE

For M – again

Il n'y a aucune bienveillance
dans l'écriture, plutôt une terreur.

Barthes

Act One

London.
   The principal room of a suite in a luxury hotel.
Doorway to main entrance. Doorway to bedroom.
   Alceste bursts through the main entrance, followed by John.

JOHN

What is it?

ALCESTE
Please leave me alone.

JOHN

                              What's wrong?
Come on – tell me what the hell's going on.

ALCESTE
Just leave me alone – I'd be eternally fucking grateful.

JOHN
You could at least listen without getting in a state.

ALCESTE

                                        I'll

decide what state to be in, thank you.

JOHN
I just don't understand you.
We're supposed to be friends, then you *pick* on me.

ALCESTE
Friends? Don't make me laugh. Our friendship is
   history.
We used to be friends – OK – correct –

but there are limits to what I'm prepared to accept.
And when I see you talking such total shit
I realise I'm dealing with just one more hypocrite.

JOHN
Alceste, don't tell me you're upset . . .

ALCESTE
Upset? That's the best understatement yet.
To do that to a man with no coercion
is a form of social perversion.
You're suddenly kissing this man on both cheeks:
'Darling – haven't seen you for *weeks* –
if there's anything you need at all
don't hesitate (or was it on his mouth) to call.'
But when I ask you what his game is
you can't even tell me what the bastard's name is.
If I was that compromised, Christ knows,
I think I'd take a fucking overdose.

JOHN (*amused*)
Suicide? Really? But isn't that the quintessent
gesture of the moody adolescent?
Will swallowing fifty paracetamol
really make the world morally more acceptable?

ALCESTE
What's that supposed to be? An example of wit?

JOHN
I'm so pleased you appreciate it.
But come on – for everyone's satisfaction –
tell us your principles of human interaction.

ALCESTE
Never try to deceive,
and only say what you truly believe.

JOHN
But if a man takes me in his arms

then I have a duty to say how charmed
I am. If he thinks we relate
then I have a moral duty to reciprocate.

What total bollocks. Nothing's more effete
than the moral contortions of the self-proclaimed
    elite.
The slobbering over the ritual greeting,
the bullshit spoken at every meeting
makes me vomit. What kind of morality
makes a fool the equal of a decent man? What kind of
    society?
OK, let's say I let myself be assaulted
by one of these people who swear I can't be faulted –
what's the point them eulogising my name
if they treat some cretin exactly the same?
I'm sorry I'm sorry but no one in their right mind
wants (or needs) that kind
of praise. That level of sycophancy
is typical of our moral bankruptcy.
If you value everyone equally highly, I'm afraid you'll
    never
have any values whatsoever.
And since you subscribe to the prevailing culture
I dissociate myself from you if as a result you're
keener to lick arses
than make discriminating choices.
I want to be *valued*. I really can't face
people whose embrace
indiscriminately includes the entire human race.

But you're part of society – and one of its norms
is to accept the customary forms
of politeness.

ALCESTE

　　　　　Politeness? I'd introduce extreme penalties
for trafficking in false loyalties.
The purpose (it seems to me) of human discourse
should be to exchange our innermost thoughts
and feelings. In other words what I'm asking
is to see the *man* speaking – not the mask.

JOHN

I can think of places where that philosophy
wouldn't get much sympathy.
Besides – with respect to your ideals –
what's wrong with sometimes hiding what you feel?
Would you really tell certain men and women
exactly what you think of them?
Go up to a fellow artist, say, and start
to tear their precious work apart?

ALCESTE

Absolutely.

JOHN

　　　　　So you'd really tell the director at this
　morning's screening
that the film was anodyne, with no political thrust
　or meaning?

ALCESTE

Definitely.

JOHN

　　　　　And I suppose you'd find that sinister
and point the finger at interference by a government
　minister.

ALCESTE

Naturally.

JOHN

You're joking.

ALCESTE

No I'm not.

Not when I've got
so many examples in front of me
of private political and artistic hypocrisy.
I'm enraged. I can't forgive
the way that men and women choose to live.
Everywhere you look: sycophants, compromise,
    hypocrites,
nepotism, betrayal, vested interests –
I've had enough. Call it insanity
but I take issue with the whole of humanity.

JOHN

I have to say that this so-called rage
would make more sense on the seventeenth-century
    stage.
And surely as a playwright you're aware
of sounding like something straight out of Molière.

ALCESTE

Jesus Christ, you think you're so clever.

JOHN

You see, you'll never
change society single-handed. And if it's the truth
    you're after,
the truth is is that ranting moralists are met by
    ridicule and laughter.

ALCESTE

Exactly. That's just what I'd expect.
It would nauseate me to be treated with respect.

JOHN

Are you saying that humanity should be condemned?

7

I'm saying that humanity as we know it – yes –
   should come to an end.

JOHN

And are we to take it (because I think you're going
   too far)
that no one is exempt from your *fatwah*?
Is it universal, or will there be some / kind of –

ALCESTE

Universal. I hate everyone.
And not just people in the public eye,
but the public themselves who just stand by
and watch – whose understanding's limited
to absorbing a few selected images.
As you know, I'm in the potentially disastrous position
of allegedly slandering this wretched politician
just by asking why his touchy-feely party's quite
so cosy with a bloated member of the European
   ultra-right.
Immediately some aide from Central Office calls:
'It's smear' she goes, 'withdraw your comment
   or we'll have your balls.'
I won't. The story's out. The Leader's head's on
   screens –
his smile's a metre wide – he's using every means
he can: his grin, his grief, his wife's downmarket –
   fashion
to fox the voters with his toxic spray-on brand of
   fake compassion:
He loves the poor – we're all in this together –
he'll save the unemployed – He cleverly
adopts a flat bland mask of pity
and never mentions once his shit-rich banking cronies
   in the City.
And by the evening so successful is he –

so smart – so very very busy
looking clean, the press get scared they might offend
and quietly drop the story of his grubby fascist friend.
Jesus wept! And you wonder why
I sometimes want to just curl up and die?
I have a dream of a clean white space
entirely disinfected of the human race.

JOHN

Please
could we just ease
up on contemporary morality
and show a little more understanding of human reality.
Wouldn't it be good to see
some flexibility?
(Or even moral relativity?)
After all, society changes,
and there are whole ranges
of valid responses. Extremes are usually dangerous
and often cause unreasonable pain to us.
We live in a complex social matrix:
nothing's solved by boring us with politics.
Perfection's beyond us. Why can't you just go
with the flow?
If you want to castigate society
then please do it well away from me.
I'm as aware as you are of people's malefactions,
they simply don't provoke the same absurd reactions.
I take people as they come. And if someone acts like
    a shit
then – OK – no problem – let's just quietly deal with it.

You know as well as I do the essential rule
is keep calm, stay cool.

ALCESTE

You're so reasonable you make me sick.

9

You'd stay cool while someone sliced off your prick.
What if a close friend betrays you?
Steals your ideas? Never repays you?
What if they sell your story to the gutter press?
Don't you seek redress?

JOHN

Perhaps. Yes.
But I don't lose my temper. It's hard to be 'enraged'
if one is philosophically disengaged.
And the human animal looks far less fearsome
through the prism
of postmodernism.
The world's a mess. Absolutely. We've fucked it.
So why not just sit back and deconstruct it?

ALCESTE

So I should allow myself to come to harm
and stay quite calm?
Words can't express my hatred of corrupt men.

JOHN

Why don't you just shut up then.

Pause.

This court case of yours, how will you influence the
  outcome?

ALCESTE

I shan't. That way the result will be all the speedier.

JOHN

But who's going to leak the dirt on him to the media?

ALCESTE

No one: no phone-taps, no long-lens / photography . . .

JOHN

So who's going to catch the judge downloading
  child-pornography?

ALCESTE
No one. I have justice on my side.

JOHN
That's the legal equivalent of suicide.

ALCESTE
No dirty tricks. The way I see it,
it's an open and / shut case.

JOHN
On your own head be it.

ALCESTE
That's fine.

JOHN
You don't seem to realise you're dealing
with an opponent whose / political power . . .

ALCESTE
I find that rather appealing.

JOHN
Well I don't.

ALCESTE
It's my right to choose.

JOHN
I don't think / that's wise.

ALCESTE
And besides I'm quite happy to lose.

JOHN
You must be / joking.

ALCESTE
Given our sick and twisted judiciary, I trust this
will become a classic example of perversion of the
    course of justice.

JOHN

You're out of your mind. This is / *insanity.*

ALCESTE

Losing my case would be a great moral victory.

JOHN

No such thing exists, Alceste. (Really, the stuff you spout
would make intelligent people just fall about.)

ALCESTE

That's their problem.

JOHN

Really? I think it could well
be yours too. But tell
me something: it seems you're not so inflexible
in your attitude to . . . sexual
partners. Not so above it all
you don't notice what's available.
Not so embroiled in your heroic struggle with the human race
you fail to recognise a pretty face.
I'm just amazed that you should admire
such an unlikely object of desire.
Ellen, I suspect, is secretly rather fascinated by you.
Marcia can hardly disguise the fact that she's infatuated by you.
But you don't even speak to them any more
since you became obsessed by Jennifer,
a woman whose distaste for monogamy
is already legendary.
And since she's arrived in London
her door's been open to men almost at random.
She flirts, she slags people off. Is that acceptable
just because she's beautiful?

Ever since she crossed the Atlantic
her life in this hotel has been both frivolous and frantic.
Surely she represents everything you most hate?

ALCESTE
She's still very young and vulnerable. Don't underrate
love. I know exactly
what her faults are and in a perverse way they attract
  me.
She takes her success at face value (but then again
that's very American)
and until she gains more insight I'm resigned
(no please don't laugh) to going out of my mind.
My strategy is to let *her* choose
when to reveal her hidden virtues.

JOHN
Hidden is certainly the operative word.
Does she love you?

ALCESTE
          Don't refer
to her like that. Of course she does.

JOHN
So then what's all this fuss
you've been making about her other boyfriends?
  Insecurity?

ALCESTE
Look: all I ask is a one-hundred-per-cent commitment
  to me.
I've simply come here for an explanation,
and to alert her to the seriousness of the situation.

JOHN
Well I'm sorry, but if you ask me,
Ellen would be a far more likely

candidate. It's the kind of opportunity not to be missed:
sex with a celebrity post-feminist journalist –
reason enough, surely, to try her.

ALCESTE
Reason has no influence over desire.

JOHN
You're beginning to worry me. Any
other man would surely . . .

He sees Covington in the doorway. Slight pause.

COVINGTON
Hello. I'd arranged to meet Jenny
here after the screening
but a message down at the desk said that now this
    evening
is the earliest she can manage. Pity.
But then they told me
(rather begrudgingly)
that you had use of the key.
(Of course that's nothing whatsoever to do with me –
I mean: the key
why should it be?
Obviously.)
But then I thought, well why not take this opportunity
of coming up to see
a man
I've always dreamed of taking by the hand
thereby confirming our friendship
and cementing – dare I say it? Yes I do – a lasting
    relationship.

*He offers his hand to Alceste, who seems unaware of
his existence.*

Excuse me, I thought we were having a conversation.

ALCESTE

Really?

COVINGTON

Or have I misread the situation?

ALCESTE

You should just be (I'm not sure) just be aware of the
    danger
of committing yourself to a complete stranger.

COVINGTON

Well I'm sorry if I startled you,
it's just I've always had the very highest regard for you.

ALCESTE

Listen –

COVINGTON

Of course (yes, don't say it) there are writers
    in more prominent positions,
but none with the breadth, depth and sheer range of
    your dramatic vision.

ALCESTE

Listen –

COVINGTON

Believe me, this comes straight from the heart
which is why I'm so anxious to start
a genuine friendship – anticipating that any future
benefits will be mutual.
Let's set up a meeting. How full's your diary?
Shall we do lunch?

ALCESTE

I'm sorry?

COVINGTON

Is there a problem? Excuse me?

ALCESTE

A problem? No. Hold on. I'm a little overwhelmed –
that's all – to be claimed as a friend
so suddenly . . . I mean without any preliminary . . .
I like there to be a little bit of . . .

(how can I put this?)

COVINGTON

Of mystery?

ALCESTE

Exactly.

COVINGTON

Of course.

ALCESTE

It takes *time* / to make –

COVINGTON

Absolutely.

ALCESTE

– the right choices. I'm afraid I'm (sorry) slightly
fanatical
about friendship. (I mean we may be / quite
incompatible.)

COVINGTON

Absolutely – you're absolutely right.
Time – yes – a characteristic, if I may say so, insight
into human nature. Brilliant. Meanwhile if there's
anything at all
you need (perhaps a little editorial?)
just call
me at the paper.

Produces card.

Or look: phone me at home.

I want you to feel that as an artist you're not alone.
We critics are artists too:
perhaps you don't realise just how much I could do
    for you.
Who knows – it might even reach the stage
where I could get you on to the front page –
like a Lloyd-Webber musical – or some other natural
    disaster.

Laughs at his own joke.

OK, OK, you're wondering what I'm after:
well the fact is I have something here
(a play actually)
a script I've been working on for the past year –
and I'd love to get your reaction.

ALCESTE (*faint laugh*)
I don't think you'll get much satisfaction
out of me.

COVINGTON
        I'm sorry?

ALCESTE
        You'll find
I have the unfashionable habit of speaking my mind.

COVINGTON
Exactly. Good. Yes. I don't want you to be nice:
I'm looking for genuine dramaturgical advice –
I mean if there's anything in particular wrong with it . . .

ALCESTE
OK, OK – shall we just get on with it?

COVINGTON
On with it?

ALCESTE
    Read it.

COVINGTON
You mean here? Now? In front of you?

ALCESTE
Here. Now. Why not? Wouldn't that be fun to do?

Alceste grins. Covington opens his script and reads.

COVINGTON
'Scene One. Evening. An attic room.' Perhaps I should
  just say
it's more a scene than a complete play.

ALCESTE
OK.

COVINGTON
'A man and a woman' – and it's directly based
on my own personal experience.

ALCESTE
Well that's often the case.

COVINGTON
Exactly. 'Scene One.' Is it? Good. (The man by the
  way is me,
there's a strong element of . . .)

ALCESTE
Autobiography.

COVINGTON
Exactly. Yes. Of course there are more scenes planned.

ALCESTE
Fine. A first draft. I understand.

COVINGTON
'Scene One. Evening. An attic room. A man and a
  woman: Clair.
Clair is young and beautiful.

The man is somewhat older – powerful
but sensitive and aware.'

ALCESTE
(Of what? Sorry? Is this the play?)

COVINGTON
Just aware.

ALCESTE
(Aware. I see. OK.)

COVINGTON
'They look at each other. Silence.'

Pause.

ALCESTE
But what are the characters' intentions?

COVINGTON
Those are just the stage directions.

ALCESTE
(OK. I see.)

JOHN
Two good strong parts.

COVINGTON
Thank you. Now this is where the dialogue starts –

'MAN My darling, let me crush you in my arms.

WOMAN I'm no longer susceptible to your monied charms.

MAN Make love to me. Forget this girlish nonsense.

WOMAN I can't. I have a new-found social conscience.

Pause.'

JOHN
Brilliant. I'm hooked. The theme is timeless.

ALCESTE

(I've never heard anything so completely / mindless.)

COVINGTON

'MAN Remember all the good times that we had.

WOMAN The times that you call good now all seem bad.

MAN Let's dine out at my restaurant. The limousine is
ready.

WOMAN I'd rather stay at home and cook my own
spaghetti.
I'd rather stay at home and find out who I am.

MAN Your name is Clair. And I'm the man
who loves you. Who cares if it's not right!

WOMAN Oh God! Oh God!

They kiss beneath the leaking skylight.'

Closes the script with satisfaction.

There's already interest from the RSC.

JOHN

I'm not surprised. I liked the pause particularly.

COVINGTON

You don't think it owes too much to Pinter?

JOHN

Far from it. There's not even a hint of . . .

ALCESTE

(Talent.)

JOHN

. . . plagiarism. In fact I don't think I appear t've
heard anything quite like it in the theatre.
Have you, Alceste?

COVINGTON (*delighted*)
Really?

ALCESTE
(What?)

COVINGTON
D'you mean it?

ALCESTE
(I pity the poor bastards who / have to read it.)

JOHN
Of *course* I mean it. The National's sure to / buy it.

COVINGTON
What d'you think, Alceste? You're being very quiet.

ALCESTE (*smiles*)
Listen. When someone writes a script
it's very hard for them to stand back from it.
I did in fact once read a scene similar to yours
(admittedly without the pause)
but it did give me cause
to wonder what makes people cover page after page
with dialogue so unplayable on the stage.
Why is there so little insight
into the qualities required to be a playwright?

COVINGTON
If you're talking about what I've just read
to you, I / think you should –

ALCESTE
That's not what I said.
No. It was more of a rhetorical question.
Listen. Let me make a suggestion:
if someone has zero facility
it's a disability
they should conceal.

COVINGTON
Zero facility? Is he talking about me?

ALCESTE
I just said 'someone'. Please don't shout. (You see –
people just have to discuss writing
and they / start fighting.)

COVINGTON
Are you saying I have no talent?

ALCESTE
I'm not saying anything. Perhaps you have – perhaps
   you haven't.
(Although you can still write total shit
and find some fool to workshop it
book a venue for the evening
and subject your friends to a rehearsed reading.)
Whatever. But please – resist the temptation:
you're not going to get an Olivier nomination
(unless of course it's your own).
As a critic you have a certain reputation –
but would you yourself enjoy critical examination?
It's much easier to face a first night
as a critic than a gibbering playwright.

COVINGTON
Yes, but specifically about my scene –
d'you mean / it's –

ALCESTE
Your scene is rubbish.

COVINGTON
              (Uh-huh. You mean the actual / scene.)

ALCESTE
The way your characters speak is stilted and unnatural.
(The actual scene, yes.)

It's flaccid. The dialogue's weak.
The acid test is to reflect the way that people really
    speak.
'Crush you in my arms'?
'Susceptible to your monied charms'?

COVINGTON

It is a first draft.

ALCESTE

And you wonder why people laughed?
Listen: if you must write a play
it helps not only to have something to say
but also a way of saying it that arrests us
engages us and tests us.
Your dialogue I'm afraid is the verbal equivalent
of industrial effluent
i.e. the tedious platitudes
of emotionally self-indulgent middle-class attitudes –
the kind of waste
that unfortunately we can't legislate against.
(So he loves her, so she's being mean. / Who gives a
    fuck?)

COVINGTON

I'm sorry, but it's a contemporary theme.

ALCESTE

If that's your idea of contemporary
you should be adapting classics for the BBC.
(Being so indifferent to good writing
they'd probably find your work rather exciting.)

John laughs.

No, I'm quite serious:
that kind of sloppy imprecision's
just what they like on television.

COVINGTON
Well I'm sorry, but I've been told it has potential.

ALCESTE
Well of course it's essential
for you to believe that.
(If you didn't want my opinion you / shouldn't've
asked for it.)

COVINGTON
It's already had several rehearsed readings.

ALCESTE
Well naturally – people are afraid of hurting / your
   feelings.

COVINGTON
Well-known actors have read these parts.

ALCESTE
Actors are generous. They have over-kind / hearts.

COVINGTON
Artists are always misunderstood.

ALCESTE
                              But the hard part is
is the misunderstood are not necessarily artists.

COVINGTON
Well I'd be very interested to see
how you'd handle a similar theme.

ALCESTE
Listen – if I *had* written such a load of crap
I wouldn't be going round advertising the fact.

COVINGTON
I'd advise you not to adopt that tone.

ALCESTE

Oh really? Listen: why don't you just leave me alone.
Go home.

COVINGTON

You're arrogant, rude and totally insensitive.

ALCESTE

And you're becoming increasingly offensive.

JOHN

Please. Both of you. What if she walks in?

COVINGTON

Who? Jennifer? Oh my God have I been
(sorry) shouting? He's right. We'll deal with this (OK?)
another day.

ALCESTE

Absolutely. And thank you so much for showing us
your play.

Covington goes.

JOHN

Congratulations. All he wanted was encouragement
and you turn it into a major incident.
Did you have to make such a big bloody deal of it?

ALCESTE

Just shut the fuck up / will you.

JOHN

Oh charming.

ALCESTE

Hypocrite.

Pause.

JOHN

I hope you realise . . .

ALCESTE
I'm not listening.

JOHN
Fine.

ALCESTE
Don't interfere.

Pause.

Realise what?

JOHN
Nothing.

ALCESTE
Tell me.

JOHN
Only that you've just ended your career.

ALCESTE
Please. I'm not prepared to discuss the topic.

JOHN
And I'm beginning to find you excessively misanthropic.

Act Two

Alceste, Jennifer.

ALCESTE
Listen: I'm afraid I'm in a mood
today to question your whole incredible attitude.
You're looking at a man at the end of his tether
who's finding it harder and harder to believe we have
    a future together.
Of course I could lie to you,
but that's something I would never do.
I can't say things I don't believe
although it would be far less painful to / deceive you.

JENNIFER
I see. So I've just come back
to listen to – what? – another moral attack?

ALCESTE
Not an attack. Please. I'm talking about your intimacy
with other men – this open-door policy
which – however much I trust you –
my own nature simply can't adjust to.

JENNIFER
Intimacy? Your imagination's hyperactive.
And would you rather I was old and unattractive?
If a man wants to offer me his regards
what do I do? Call in my bodyguards?

ALCESTE
That's not the point. Clearly you will attract men:
the mistake is to actively encourage them.
The kind of signals you emit

give the impression – how shall I put it? –
that you're fair game.
I'm sorry but it's true. I'm not saying I blame
you (please, that's not what I meant)
but to claim your behaviour's innocent
is certainly contentious
(and probably disingenuous).
Perhaps you'd like to explain
for example why again and again
I find Alexander here. I have great difficulty seeing
why you think he's such a wonderful human being.
Unless that year-round orange tan
is something you find appealing, is it, in a man?
Perhaps you don't find it odd
he's always staring at some part of a woman's body?
I suppose his loft in Covent Garden
is a real come on:
not only has he got those sharks in tanks he's
also invested heavily in Banksys –
gets girls to appreciate his kitsch effects –
then drags them off for unprotected sex.

JENNIFER (*laughing*)
That's *not true*.
For Christsake Alceste, what the hell's gotten into you?
Alex is my agent. He'd sooner I signed a contract
than attempt high-risk physical contact.

ALCESTE
Then why can't your 'agent' leave you alone?
Why can't he deal with you on the phone?

JENNIFER
You seem to be jealous of the entire male race.

ALCESTE
Well hasn't the entire male race been invited up to this
    place?

28

JENNIFER

You ought to find that reassuring.
Isn't it just plain boring
to see so many men? Wouldn't it be much more exciting
if there was a favourite I kept on inviting?

ALCESTE

The favourite is supposed to be me.
(And you wonder why I'm going mad / with jealousy.)

JENNIFER

I love you, Alceste. Isn't that enough?

ALCESTE

That's just a word I'm afraid: 'love'.

JENNIFER

Well it's a word I don't use lightly.
(Really I'm not interested in your linguistic / snobbery.)

ALCESTE

Don't use lightly. Please. Come *on*.
You probably say it to everyone.

JENNIFER

Thank you, Alceste. Thank you so much.
Thank you for your kindness, respect and trust.
How charming. But I refuse to be upset.
Let's just say that as far as my love goes, you can
    forget
it. That way no one can deceive
you but yourself.

ALCESTE

                Jesus wept, I don't believe
this. I'd like to tear my obsession
out by the roots. Let me confess
something: d'you think I'm remotely pleased
to be in the grip of this disease-

like thing: love? I hate this role:
this humiliating lack of self-esteem and self-control.

Really? Aren't you used to having feelings?

Not when it means dealing
with you, no. My love is incandescent.
I won't be treated like an infatuated adolescent.

I don't understand. Would you rather pick a fight
    with me
or spend the night with me?
You say love, but what you seem
to have in mind's a kind of puritanical *régime*.

Phone.

If you would just – please – stop playing
games, perhaps we could find a way of saying
what we really / feel . . . (Oh Jesus, I give up.)

JENNIFER (*picks up phone*)
Yes? Who is it? Oh, hi! (It's Julian.) No. Come right up.

I thought you wanted to talk
but no – now some arsehole is going to just walk
in here uninvited. Couldn't it wait? Is it so hard to say
to someone: 'No, come back later'?

Julian wouldn't appreciate that.

Julian is a spoilt egotistical overrated showbiz brat.

JENNIFER

Well exactly. He knows so many people
that offending him's a potentially lethal / exercise.

ALCESTE

So now you're going to flatter / his ego by –

JENNIFER

Please. Don't pretend these things don't matter.
I'm frightened he could interfere
with the natural progression of my career
if I start saying no. These people never manage to do
anything useful – but they can damage you.
To make some kind of issue of it would be insane
(and besides he supplies me with cocaine).

Phone.

ALCESTE

Yes yes yes. Always some excuse not to be alone
with me. And now – Jesus Christ – it's the phone
again. There's absolutely no / *privacy.* I thought we'd
    agreed.

JENNIFER *(picks up phone)*

Oh hi! Alexander. How *are* you? Come right up.

ALCESTE *(makes to go)*

Alexander. That's all I need.

JENNIFER

Where're you going?

ALCESTE

Out.

JENNIFER

Please stay.

ALCESTE

And be humiliated?

31

JENNIFER

But Alceste.

ALCESTE

No.

JENNIFER

Please.

ALCESTE

I'm sorry but I'm not affiliated
to this particular club.

JENNIFER

But just for today.

ALCESTE

You're being absurd.

JENNIFER

How? By asking you to stay?
Why? Is it so unreasonable to request
just a modicum maybe of graciousness?

ALCESTE

Sit there, you mean, and listen to their trivia.

JENNIFER

Please. For me.

ALCESTE

I've said no.

JENNIFER

Just go then if you're so fucking superior.

*They realise that Julian and Alexander along with
John and Ellen have appeared and witnessed the end
of the argument. Brief silence.*

ELLEN

We met this pair in the lobby.

JENNIFER
Ellen. How *are* you?

They kiss.

ELLEN
Are we still OK for the interview?

JENNIFER
Absolutely. Looking forward to it.
Julian. Alex. Hi! Can I put you two on hold for just
a minute?

She takes Alceste aside.

So. Are you staying?

ALCESTE
Only if you stop this degrading game-playing.

JENNIFER
Please shut up.

ALCESTE
Then state your position.

JENNIFER
You're being embarrassing.

ALCESTE
Then make a decision.

JENNIFER
A *what*?

ALCESTE
Yes. Them or me.

JENNIFER
You are joking.

ALCESTE
Not at all. You forget I'm not frightened of provoking /
your pet celebrities.

Alceste moves away as Alex comes up and kisses Jennifer.

ALEX

Well fuck and fuck again – I've just fucked up a
    crucial deal
by offering Tony bread-rolls to have with our meal.
Not only does he have this list of things he will not eat
– like sesame shellfish peas nuts milk cheese sugar
    toffee coffee bread or anything containing wheat –
but when I dare to call this global food-intolerance in
    doubt
bangs down his plate and fuck – he's gone – the man
    walks out!

JENNIFER

That's so typical. Tony's an object-lesson in narcissistic
    self-obsession.
And since the move to LA he's a born-again
low-carb high-maintenance hysterical Californian.

JULIAN

Talking of self-obsession, I've just spent the last
hour on the phone with Debbie in tears. She just
can't come to terms with the plain
fact that her career is over. But what can you say?

JENNIFER

Julian – you're too kind-hearted.
From what I hear it never even started.
The woman's thirty-two and yet
she's still waiting to be offered Juliet.

JULIAN (*laughs*)

(Oh you bitch.)

JENNIFER

(She *told* me.)

34

ELLEN (*switches on her recording machine*)
Is it OK to quote you on that?

JENNIFER
I'm sorry? Quote what you like, Ellen. It's a fact.

Laughter.

ELLEN
Was it exciting to meet Philip?

JENNIFER
We had an interesting, shall we say, relationship.
But that's okay – I'm so past the stage
of caring when a man – what? – three times my age
hits on me. I'm just really really pleased to see
him promoting all that home-grown talent on TV –
doing that thing where any vulnerable girl's allowed
to sing like shit if it'll please the crowd.
So – sure – Phil's cool – nice teeth, big mouth – not deep
but kind of special: he's a total creep.

Laughter.

ELLEN
What about Jeanette?

JENNIFER
                    What can I say?
Jeanette is one of the bravest women working in the
    business today.
At least that's what I read
in all your papers – about how she's succeeded
in giving a voice to whatever – to minorities.
But I have it on good authority
her secret homophobia's so intense
she won't be photographed or even seen at gay events.

ELLEN
Can you comment on her relationship with Leavis?

35

JENNIFER

Comment? I could write you an entire thesis.
Now there's an editor with no imagination
who's managed to carve out a reputation
for being at the cutting edge
by draining meaning out of life and language.
As respected critics get the axe
they're rapidly replaced by brat-pack hacks
paid to indulge her burning passion
for Hollywood, consumer goods and fashion.
She sets the limits of discourse
at this star's sexuality, and that one's fourth divorce.
Ethnic violence, murderous outrages
are strictly banished from her modish pages –
unless of course some supermodels on a hack-job
are looking for a war zone as a backdrop.
But hey – I wouldn't set myself above it –
her magazine is great – I love it.

Laughter.

ELLEN

What was it like to work with Morris?

JENNIFER

Abominable.
He thinks of himself as the Delphic fucking oracle –
imagines he's the height of moral bravery
for writing scripts that deal with genocide and slavery –
believes he's wise – but what he's done is crossed
the feel-good factor with the holocaust.

Laughter.

ELLEN

How about Clair? Have you been?
I know people rave about her cuisine.

JENNIFER

That's right: she collects exotic recipes
and is rightly famous for her dinner parties.

ALEX

I always say it is impossible to beat
the way that woman, frankly, handles meat:
her flambéed *escalopes* are truly amazing.

JENNIFER

If only her intellect were equally blazing.
The most interesting subject simply sparks
off a string of totally banal remarks.

Laughter.

ELLEN

I believe you know Simon.

JENNIFER

Yes. Why? Simon is a personal friend of mine.

JOHN

I've heard he's extremely bright.

JENNIFER

So bright he'll spend half the night
proving it. Do you *believe* a man
who speaks entirely in epigrams.
Poor Simon. He can't relax. He's ineffectual
because his responses are purely intellectual.
I doubt that he could make *love* to me
without supplying a critical commentary
with footnotes. And when he's taken coke
he starts to babble on about the *baroque*
and how it would've been such ecstasy
to've lived in a previous century
and all that shit. How nothing written today

37

compares to the music of Lully or Marin Marais
blah blah blah. Which is when of course he starts to
    fumble at my dress
– and promptly loses consciousness.

Laughter.

                    JULIAN (*with admiration*)
That's Simon so exactly. *God* she's a bitch.

                    ALEX
What you have there, Jenny, is a very special gift.

                    ALCESTE
That's it. Go on. I notice your attacks
are only made behind people's backs.
If those people walked into this room
now you'd soon
be all over them with darling this
and darling fucking that.

                    ALEX
Don't accuse us of hypocrisy:
speak to our resident celebrity.

                    ALCESTE
But it's you and your entourage
who encourage
her. It's your pseudo-conviviality
that feeds her taste for this point-scoring triviality.
She might be less sarcastic
if she was deprived of her enthusiastic
audience. Flattery
destroys an individual's critical faculty.

                    JOHN
But doesn't this all sound rather familiar?
Aren't your pet hates actually rather similar?

JENNIFER

Yes, but contradiction is
this man's *vocation*. His
reputation is such that he'd
lose face if he was seen to agree
with anyone – let alone me.
He's so in love with the idea of a fight
that the left half of his brain is at odds with the right.
And if someone *else* expresses an opinion he shares,
    then that's it:
he attacks it.

Laughter.

ALCESTE

Yes, yes – very funny. But then in this company I'd be
    surprised
not to find myself satirised.

JOHN

But come on: admit
you're genetically predisposed to contradict.
It's a sickness. He gets equally mad
if you call something good or the same thing bad.

ALCESTE

That's because people are always wrong.
The sickness is they've no idea what's really going on.
Their critical criteria are rubbish. All
their judgements are entirely superficial.

JENNIFER

Oh, *please* . . .

ALCESTE

Please what? Don't you realise
you're just an amusing object in these men's eyes?
OK. It's very entertaining. But you should try
asking what they say about you in private.

ALEX (*smoothly*)

Listen: it would be neither professional nor gallant –
he's lying, sweetheart – for me to rubbish my own best
  client.

JULIAN

What can I say?
You know we all love you. You're a babe.

ALCESTE

Don't you see they're just bullshitting you?
I may be upsetting you
but at least that's a function of my sincerity.
I hate to see
you living at this skin-deep level
never taking the time or trouble
to question what your life's really about.
I mean why can't you just throw these people *out*?

JENNIFER (*upset*)

Sincerity? Don't you just mean
you want to make an unpleasant scene?
Your programme of instruction apparently depends
on insulting both myself and my closest friends.

To Ellen.

Are you still taping this?

ELLEN

If you don't mind. I think it's shaping
into a very interesting piece,
and it's the unguarded moments like these
that are so revealing
about what my subjects are really experiencing and
  feeling.
If I didn't believe you were the new female icon
I wouldn't've dared to leave the mic on –
but you see I find your sexual politics

fascinating. It seems the trick is
to surround yourself with men
and yet have no specific psychosexual need for them.
Am I right? And of course you don't have to answer me
but I also get this so so weird seventeenth-century
feel from all of this. It's like I'm in a room of stock
characters. It's not postmodern, it's *baroque*.
It's quite unsettling, but then again
perhaps this is the style of the new millennium:
a pre-enlightenment sense of linguistic formality
coupled with post-post-industrial virtual reality.

Everyone looks at her.

(. . . Or something like that.)

ALCESTE
Well if you want my opinion . . .

JENNIFER
Haven't we already had it?

ALCESTE
I beg your pardon?

JENNIFER
Has anyone seen the wonderful roof garden?

To Alex and Julian.

What, are you leaving?

JULIAN
Are we?

ALEX
Of course not.

ALCESTE (*to Jennifer*)
That would put you in something of a spot
wouldn't it. It would mean you were free
to speak to me.

JULIAN
I've nothing till later this afternoon.
What about you? Are you going soon?

ALEX
Me? I don't need to get away
until our office opens in LA.

JULIAN
(When's that?)

ALEX
(Four p.m. our time.)
Phone.

JENNIFER (*over previous two lines*)
Why are you behaving like this?

ALCESTE
I'm just trying to test your priorities.

JENNIFER (*picks up phone*)
Yes? Hello? I see. So he's on his way.
OK.
It seems there's a young man in a leather jacket
coming up to deliver an urgent packet
to Alceste.

ALCESTE
I don't think that's at all likely.

JENNIFER
But he asked for you at the desk – one of these . . .
    motorcycle
people . . .

ELLEN
Courier.

JENNIFER
Courier. Thank you.

The Messenger appears – long hair, beard, leathers.

Oh my
he's here already. (*To Alceste.*) Now just try
and be nice to him.

MESSENGER
Package for Alceste.

ALEX
Please. Come in.

MESSENGER
If you could just sign here and print your name before
  you take . . .

ALCESTE (*doing so*)
OK, OK. Are you sure this isn't a mistake?

*He signs and takes the 'package' – a letter – to one
side, opens it and reads. Jennifer meanwhile intercepts
the Messenger.*

JENNIFER
Don't you get hot in all that leather?

MESSENGER
Depends. Y'know. On the weather.

ALCESTE
Jesus wept.

JULIAN
Bad news?

ALCESTE
I don't believe it.

To John.

Just look at that. The bastard. Take it. Read it.

John takes the letter.

43

JENNIFER (*takes Messenger's arm*)
What is this? You're upsetting our visitor.

JOHN (*faint laugh*)
I don't understand. It's from Covington's solicitor.
He's threatening to sue for defamation . . .

JENNIFER
Have I missed something?

JOHN
. . . unless he gets a full retraction
of the quote 'malicious attack' unquote on his play
in progress.

ALCESTE
He's not going to get away
with this.

JOHN
He claims to be suffering mental distress
and loss of earnings as a direct consequence.

JENNIFER
You mean Covington the *critic?*
That's ridic-
ulous.

JOHN
Nevertheless it might be sensible to compromise.

ALCESTE
What? You want me to tell lies?
I'm going to fight.
This is a man who destroys writers' reputations
    overnight.
Mental distress? No way will I praise
his crappy little stabs at writing so-called plays.

JOHN
I still think you should / calm down.

44

MESSENGER
Uh . . . Is there a reply?

ALCESTE
Yes there is. Tell him I'd rather die
than retract. And you can pass on
the message that his reviews aren't fit to wipe my
    arse on.

To Alex and Julian, who are trying not to laugh.

And perhaps you two would like to explain
just what you both find so / entertaining.

MESSENGER
So. OK. Shall I wait while you / write that down?

ALCESTE (*to Jennifer*)
And don't think I've forgot-
ten our previous conversation. (*To Messenger.*) What?

MESSENGER
I said: shall I wait while you write that down?

ALCESTE
No. You can find another helmet and bike me into
    town.

45

Act Three

Alexander, Julian.

ALEX
You always look so unconcerned.
I wish I could've learned
that little trick. You're like some almost very very
    boring
gorgeous early Andy Warhol drawing –
I'm fascinated. Are you really blessed
with perfect equanimity? Don't you ever get depressed?

JULIAN
What about?

ALEX
(Because I do.)

JULIAN
                    There's no secret:
what you see, Alex, is what you get.
Mummy's famous – so is Dad. Of course I've taken
    some trouble
to get noticed – but it's hardly been a struggle.
The transition from teenage idol
to stage and film was painless, so I think I'm entitled
to feel fairly pleased with myself:
I've got work, women, prestige, *ridiculous* (at my age)
    wealth.
I've experimented with guilt, but I'm afraid self-doubt
just doesn't suit me. I'm bright, I'm talked about,
and I have got talent

(and I could name others in my position who haven't).
Basically what it means
is I've inherited all the useful genes
get all the attention in my scenes
and feature regularly in the Sunday magazines.
Worrying about what to wear is the closest
I ever come to what might be called neurosis.
Oh – and my teeth: if I do have a failing
it's my obsession with a three-monthly clean and
    descaling.
But depression? You're joking. I wouldn't want to be
anything other than what I am. (I have no problems
    mentally.)

ALEX

Nevertheless you appear
to be wasting your time here.

JULIAN

D'you really think so? No, I don't invest
my energy unless I'm confident of success.
I'm not one of these pathetic men
who thoroughly degrade themselves when
it comes to women. Anguish
and so on is not my style. The language
of love – let's face it –
is really pretty bloody basic.
I'm making an investment here and expect to earn
a very comfortable return.
I gamble – of course – but I always win:
I always take out more than I put in
(if you get my meaning) – and the clincher
is: to sleep with me would be something of a coup for
    her.
But what about you? I bet you're
after her yourself, you old lecher.

47

ALEX

I take a purely paternal interest.

JULIAN

Oh yes? And does that extend to incest?

Both laugh.

ALEX

OK. But I still think you're being rather blinkered.
I'd advise you to think hard
about this.

JULIAN

Blinkered? Oh, absolutely.

ALEX

Jennifer's – listen – very astute. She
gives nothing away – unless she's said . . .

JULIAN

What?

ALEX

. . . something to you. Has she?

JULIAN

Only 'come to bed'.

ALEX

Bullshit.

JULIAN

Well that was the implication.

ALEX

Implication bullshit. It's all in your imagination.
No – are you *serious*?

JULIAN

I'm as serious as you are.

ALEX

Stop. Listen. This isn't getting either of us very far.
Are you fucking her – or not?

Pause.

JULIAN

Not.

ALEX

OK.

JULIAN

Lunch is as far as I've got –
even then she turned up late
and spent the whole hour pushing steamed broccoli
  round her plate.

ALEX

Then listen: you're a betting man
aren't you. Yes? OK, then here's the plan:
prove to me you've had her – your word is sufficient –
and I'll waive my next six months' commission.
But, if you're the loser
and I seduce her,
then I pay my next six months' rent
by taking an additional ten per cent.
Do we have an agreement?

JULIAN

But that's obscene. How can you put such a disgusting
  take on it?
I couldn't. No. (*Lowers voice.*) She's coming. OK.
  Quick, let's shake on it.

They shake hands as Jennifer enters.

Hi.

JENNIFER
So. What are you two up to?

ALEX
Oh. Nothing.

JENNIFER
Is that why Julian's blushing?

Pause. Phone.

Excuse me.

JULIAN (*sotto voce*)
Have I gone really red?

ALEX (*sotto voce*)
Idiot.

JENNIFER (*picks up phone*)
Hello? Well stop her. Say I'm sick in bed
or something. OK, OK, I realise it's not your fault.

ALEX
Is there a problem?

JENNIFER
It seems that Marcia's called
and is on her way up here. I gave express
instructions she wasn't to get past the front desk.

JULIAN
I'm out of here. That woman's unbearable.
Alex, are you coming?

JENNIFER
That's not very charitable.
Surely you're not leaving when
you know how much she enjoys the company of
   bright young men?
She probably knows you're here –

how's she going to feel if you just up and disappear?
No wonder she's incredibly bitter
if this is the way you're going to treat her.
This is a woman who's lonely and damaged,
who's never even managed
to keep a partner. She needs therapy
but hides instead behind an ideology
of outmoded feminist
rhetoric.
And because Alceste once kissed
her (they were both drunk) at an opening night
party, she now thinks she has some kind of right
over him – which is basically why she hates me
and tries to stir up serious shit against me.
I used to respect her as a teacher – but there's a glitch –
she's become a totally intolerable malicious . . .

Marcia appears.

                                                    . . . which
way did you come up? Security
only just this minute got in touch with me.

They kiss.

MARCIA
The stairs, darling – does wonders for the calves and
    thighs.

JENNIFER
But this is such a wonderful surprise!

The men slip out.

MARCIA
Don't they believe in protocol?

JENNIFER
Drink?

No thank you. You know I never touch alcohol.

Jennifer pours herself a big drink.

Jenny, I've always (as you know) had a great deal of
    respect for you
which is why I'm not afraid to be direct with you
about your work. When I taught you at Juilliard
you were the star student. It wasn't hard
to predict your success. But what really struck
    everybody
was your fantastic integrity.
But since this last film's come out, there are influential
    (as I'm sure you know) voices
highly critical of your artistic choices,
and I've learned
enough to be really rather deeply concerned.
People are saying (and if you knew how much it hurts
    me)
that what you're doing is just one step from
    pornography.
Yes. They're saying you're an artistic coward
to consistently play women who are disempowered –
that your taste for naked flesh seems
undaunted by the most abhorrent sex scenes,
in which you're either passive or psychotic.
Of course I pointed out that what you're doing is
    erotic
not exploitative. But I sensed
they weren't too convinced by that defence.
And although I far from agreed
I did (under the most enormous pressure) have to
    concede
that your image on the screen
may be (possibly) undermining women's self-esteem,
that they have a right (yes) to be disappointed

if you even *appear* to be exploited,
that your style of living
(I mean look at it)
is not an appropriate model for today's women.
Listen: I'm not saying you've sold out,
I'm just saying I'm worried about
you. You're not corrupt, but be aware that you're
entering a morally grey area.
I know that you're sufficiently intelligent
to realise that this advice is well meant.
And I wouldn't've even mentioned it
if I didn't feel we had a very special relationship.

JENNIFER
Well thank you, Marcia. You've given me a great deal
to think about. And I feel
that far from taking offence (as one might) at what
    you say,
I'd prefer to instantly return the favour.
And since you've shown such great integrity
by repeating what's said about me,
the very least that I can do
is repeat (much as it pains me) what people say about
    you.
I threw a party here the other night for intellectuals
(including I may say radical homosexuals
of both camps). And I hope I'm not betraying
    anyone's trust
to say that you were discussed.
People said that your attitude to (so-called) pornography
would be funny
if it wasn't so deeply reactionary.
They attributed your need to criticise and interfere
to the exemplary mediocrity (I think that was the
    phrase) of your own career
and suggested that jealousy

53

and confused sexuality
might be at the root of what they called the banality
of your opinions. *Professionally* you were accused of
    muscling in
on actors' work (like Lee Strasberg did to Marilyn)
– trying to maintain a niche
for the discredited techniques you teach.
It was so distressing to hear you abused –
particularly when the word 'dinosaur' was used.
Someone suggested (surely in error)
that the scenes you condemn in the movies are the ones
    you'd like to see in your own bedroom mirror.
They even mentioned your lack of prudence
in attempting to seduce your more vulnerable students,
and could only imagine that this must be
the what? – the legacy of Stanislavksi?
Naturally I leapt to your defence
and tried to prevent this (my God it was *intense*)
onslaught from developing. But I was a lone
voice. (And the tone
was far from friendly,
believe me.)
They felt that you lacked insight
and acted principally out of spite.
They claimed your long-standing grudge meant
you were disqualified from objective judgement.
So maybe it would be (don't you think) wise
to be a little less quick in future to criticise?
I *think* that you're sufficiently intelligent to realise that
this advice is well meant.
And I wouldn't've even mentioned it
if I didn't feel we had a very special relationship.

MARCIA

Of course I expected
insults, but not to be subjected

54

to this. I'm all the more disturbed,
Jennifer, because I've so obviously touched a nerve.

JENNIFER

Oh really? No, I think we should start
to have these heart-to-hearts
more regularly. Far from being frightening
I find it very very enlightening.
Let's make a deal:
how would you feel
if we agreed
to always report what's said about you and what's
    said about me?

MARCIA

What? Act as your private detective
in return for more lies and invective?

JENNIFER

You see, I'm sure the moral values we apply
undergo subtle changes as the years roll by.
And what one person sees as a celebration
of the body, another sees as cynical exploitation.
Perhaps the work I do now will seem outrageous
when I've reached middle age as
you've done, and have a chance to reassess.
I do appreciate your maternal interest:
but the fact is why should I have to listen to you?
I'm me – I'm who I am – I'm free – I'm twenty-two.

MARCIA

Age is irrelevant. This society
is a male-led *as you well know* capitalist conspiracy
which undervalues woman's function
except as teenage objects for immediate sexual
    consumption
on every poster and magazine cover.

Besides, what makes you think I'm old enough to be
  your mother?

What makes *you* think you have a right
to even be here? As it is I'm being polite,
but I could pick up that phone
and have you thrown
out. Yes. Don't you see: you are totally alone.

Pause.

I am the complete focus of all attention.
And if for reasons too . . . unbearable to mention
you can't handle it, I'm sorry. But the media's
fascination with me isn't my fault. They need an
icon. I provide it. And as for my body,
I intend to remain its sole authority.
If your own is subject to the influence of time,
then that's your problem, I'm afraid, not mine.

MARCIA
I never thought I'd live to see the day
Jennifer when you could talk that way
about a friend. Throw me out?
Listen young lady, it's about
time you confronted one or two home truths
about your career. I'm afraid you stand to lose
not just your integrity
and your dignity
but also any vestige of personal privacy.
Who's really in control? Can't you see you've been
sucked into the publicity machine
and spat out as pure product?
Are you really so completely mind-fucked
as to think there's some connection between your
  fame and your own ability?
No, you're just a brand of femininity

56

to be sold. Your face
is just one more image in the market-place,
and your body
is pure commodity.
Stars aren't born, my darling, they're made
in the world of capital and trade.
The question's not whether your name's up in lights,
the question is: who owns the rights?

But if it's so easy to become a star
then how very strange it is that you are
a what? A nobody?

Careful,
or I shall be forced to descend to your level.

Alceste enters, unseen by the two women.

Oh I know I'm not welcome here
and you'd prefer me – like your conscience – to just
    disappear.

JENNIFER (*sees Alceste*)
Not welcome? But it's been delightful.
You are a true friend. Alceste, she's so insightful
and what I particularly admire
is that very special wisdom you can only acquire
with age.

*She puts her arms around them both and leads them
downstage.*

          Listen, do promise me you'll both be wearing
the wonderful costumes I've been preparing
for this evening's little party. The theme's Louis
    Quatorze –
the kind of thing an American in Europe just adores.

Pause.

Look, why don't I leave the two of you to have a talk.
It's four o'clock. I promised I'd call my parents in
  New York.

Jennifer goes into the bedroom. Silence.

MARCIA (*faint laugh*)
Louis Quatorze?
In the old days this would be the scene where I wait
  for my carriage
while we discuss things like 'love' and 'marriage'.

Pause.

I can't tell you how much your work means
to me. You write the kinds of scenes
that mysteriously reveal the human
condition. And particularly as a woman
I feel drawn to you. I only wish
your work was better known. Rubbish
gets all the attention. You ought to be a household
  name.

ALCESTE
I like to think I have a modicum of fame.
And for the moment
at least, it's proportional to my actual achievement.

MARCIA
But you're much too modest. People get famous
for achieving far less.
A real artist like yourself may not know how to seize
the relevant opportunities
which I / might be able –

ALCESTE
Please God, don't let's start
a conversation about what is or is not art.

Besides, what major institution
isn't in a state of abject aesthetic confusion?

MARCIA

Yes, but true art makes its own conditions.
I know people in powerful positions
who speak very highly of you –
no – really – they do.

ALCESTE

People will speak highly of a pile of shit
if they've dressed up and spent fifty quid to see it.
I mean could you really bear
to sit through another play by Stoppard or Sir David
    fucking Hare?
Or watch an audience gratefully reacting
to yet another *tour de force* of classic over-acting?

(*C'est un scélérat qui parle.*)

MARCIA

Be careful who you attack.
(Is it legal to use real people's names like that?)
No, you'd be surprised
at who I know. Without being at all compromised
you're welcome to use
my connections in any way you choose.

ALCESTE

I'm afraid what you're
suggesting is anathema.
I just haven't been designed
to get down on my knees and lick unwiped behinds.

Marcia makes a face.

You see: if what I say disgusts
you then how could you possibly trust
me with your friends. When I select an epithet

59

I'm not concerned with things like etiquette.
My chronic inability to dissimulate
means it's my fate
to be excluded from the centres of power
with all the advantages they can confer.
So – yes – I break the rules,
but at least I don't have to suffer the company of fools.

MARCIA

Yes. Well. I see it's a sensitive subject.
What interests me more is what exactly is the object
of your visits here? I assume you're not . . .
    emotionally
involved? If so you've no notion
of what you're dealing with. A man with your panache
deserves better than a piece of transatlantic trash.

ALCESTE

That's an extraordinary thing to say
about someone you claim
as a friend.

MARCIA

            Perhaps. Only I'm concerned
you're going to get your fingers very badly burned.
It hurts me to see you so obsessed
when you're not (as you probably know) her principal
    interest.

ALCESTE

What's that supposed to mean?
What exactly has she been / saying to you?

MARCIA

She may be my friend, but that doesn't make her
yours, darling. She's all on the surface. Don't take her
at face value.

ALCESTE

I refuse to believe she's intrinsically shallow:
my mind's made up – and however strange it
seems to you, nothing will change it.

MARCIA

Fair enough. I'll draw my own conclusions
then and leave you to your romantic illusions.

ALCESTE

Come back. No. Marcia.
Wait. What can you do to substantiate
your accusations? You can't plant the seeds of doubt
like that and just walk out.

MARCIA

Can't I?

Pause.

Alright. Then step this way
and I'll show you my exhibit A.
Come back to my flat with me
and you'll find out everything you ever needed to
    know about infidelity
(hers I mean) but were afraid to ask.
Come on. The world's not going to fall apart.
But if it does I'll offer you what consolation
I can by way of compensation.

Act Four

Ellen, John.

JOHN
It was the most incredible sight:
he jumps off the motorbike – right? –
and immediately starts hammering on Covington's
  door.
Covington appears in shock at the first-floor
window and tells him to fuck off or he'll call the police
(I'm parked at the end of the street just in case).
Alceste says, 'You told me to call you at home
you bastard, and here I am.' 'I'm phoning
them now,' says Covington. Slams the window shut.
  Silence.
There's this feeling of potential violence.
Then the door opens: Covington grins
(a new tactic) says, 'Listen, why don't you come in
and discuss this.' (Although the door's still on the
  chain.)
'No,' says Alceste. 'I'll say what I have to say
out here. I've nothing against you as a man
or as a journalist – I've even been a fan
of yours in that capacity –
but please have the sagacity
to see that writing reviews is a world apart
from writing plays – which is: Art.
I gave you my sincere opinion, and issuing a writ
against me isn't going to alter it.'
Well Covington looks as if he's going to burst
into tears. Perhaps that's why Alceste

becomes amazingly (for him) polite.
'Let's shake hands,' he says. 'It's not dignified
to turn this into a vendetta.
After all, your play does have almost infinite potential
    to be better.'

Ellen laughs.

Poor Covington can't argue any more but
quickly shakes his hand and clicks the door shut.

ELLEN
He certainly knows how to create a scene.
It's almost touching – d'you know what I mean? –
for a man still to believe that words like 'dignified'
are not just signs, that what is signified
by 'love' or 'sincerely'
can exist independently of literary theory.

JOHN
Yes, and he's particularly Quixotic
in the way he sentimentalises the erotic.
His attitude to gender shows no respect
for any of the more important texts.
He still treats Jenny
as if she was his own personal property.

ELLEN
I know. It's shocking.
I sometimes wonder if he's mocking
us: seeing just how far he can go
with a perfect simulacrum of machismo.

JOHN
D'you think she believes in 'love' as such?

ELLEN
Jenny? I don't think she 'believes' in much
at all. She's far too intelligent

not to question –
but at the same time far too confused
to see the subtle ways in which she's being abused.

JOHN

It worries me to see *him* drawn in
to this situation. I've tried to warn him
off. I even suggested – just as an experiment –
that he might well benefit –
I suppose as a kind of re-education –
from having a relationship
with you.

ELLEN (*amused*)

Really? Do you always recommend me
then for sexual therapy?
Listen: what the two of them get up to
is their business. Yes, I'd love to
see them both happy at least
(although I am in the process of publishing a piece
which suggests that's unlikely). But as
for offering myself as a consolation prize,
experimentally or otherwise,
I'm not
sure that I've got
the nerve to be that pro-active
(nor, I have to say, do I find him remotely attractive).

JOHN

Well just be warned. In his present
state of mind he's likely to resent
any hint of rejection. And to me
you look like perfect material for his next obsessive
    fantasy.
Of course things may still work out between them
in which case we may even see them
an item yet. And if they do become a pair
then assuming you're not involved elsewhere

and can commit to it intellectually,
perhaps the two of us could . . .

ELLEN (*amused*)
Could *what*? Are you coming on to me?

JOHN
Now that's a question
I'd rather was answered by a semiotician.
To do it justice we'd really need to start
a dialogue with Derrida or Roland Barthes.

*They're both laughing as Alceste enters in intense but
suppressed rage.*

ALCESTE
Where is she?
How dare she
humiliate me.

ELLEN
It's not the end of the world already?

ALCESTE
The end of the world would be
preferable . . . I'm going to do something violent
in a moment.
Where the hell is she? (I can't even *think* / straight.)

ELLEN
I'm afraid she's not here. Calm down.
                    Get him a drink for / Godsake.

ALCESTE
How can someone so beautiful
have no sense at all of what is moral?

ELLEN
What? Is there a / connection?

ALCESTE
                    It's a total inversion

of values. It's disgusting. It's perversion.
Jennifer. After all the assurances she gave me . . .
Jennifer. Jennifer. Jennifer has betrayed me.

ELLEN
Isn't this all rather possessive?

JOHN (*hands Alceste a drink*)
Please don't be so aggressive.
Come on now. Perversion? What is this?

ALCESTE
Why don't you just mind your own fucking business.

Gulps the drink.

I've just been made to listen to her own profession
of guilt – a confession
(if you can possibly imagine a woman loving him)
of her relationship – yes – with Covington.
The man I thought she found so numbingly boring
turns out to be chief client of her compulsive whoring.

JOHN
Using that kind of language
can only exacerbate – don't you see – the damage.

ALCESTE
Don't tell me Mr Self-Abuse
the words I can or cannot use.

ELLEN
But he's right. This vocabulary is problematic.

ALCESTE
OK then. Let's stop talking and get pragmatic.
If she's capable of gross betrayal
and all the pain that entails,
I'm prepared to reciprocate –
assuming it's not too late
that is to take up your offer.

66

ELLEN (*glancing at John*)
Offer? I'm sorry?

ALCESTE
To become my lover.
John's right. A calculated gesture
like that will really test her
nerve. When she sees me transfer my attention
onto you she'll regret ever seeing that unmentionable
    little man.
Sweet revenge. You're right. It's the perfect plan.

A slight pause as Alceste pours himself another drink.
He continues to drink heavily throughout this act.

ELLEN
Listen . . . I realise you're upset. But that said
(and maybe the drink's gone to your head
or whatever) I'm not aware of any such 'plan'.
Unless John (what exactly have you been saying?) can
perhaps elucidate?
(Thank you so much, John.) But at any rate
surely this so-called 'love' of yours
should make you blind to whatever flaws
she may have. Isn't that what every cliché teaches us
from Marcel Proust back to Lucretius?

ALCESTE
There's no question of forgiving her.
This is life, not literature.
I intend to make
a complete break.

He drinks, self-absorbed, and doesn't notice that
Jennifer is in the room looking questioningly at Ellen
and John.

ELLEN (*quietly amused, to Jennifer*)
Things seem to be more than he can bear.

67

JOHN

Come on. Let's see what we're going to wear.

As they go out.

Look, I'm so sorry if I embarrassed you . . .

ELLEN

Don't worry I was just a little bit surprised, that's
   all . . .

*They've gone, laughing softly. Jennifer comes right
into the room. Alceste, of course, now knows she's
there, but remains punishingly silent, nursing his drink.*

JENNIFER

Has something happened? Are you angry?
I get the impression you're mad at me.

ALCESTE

(Give me strength.)

JENNIFER
                    I'm sorry?

ALCESTE
                              I said:
Give me strength. So what's he like in bed?

JENNIFER

What?

ALCESTE

     Still critical? Or does he lose his objectivity
during exquisite sexual activity?
Is that really all that 'love' meant?
I'm beginning to find you physically and morally
   repugnant.

JENNIFER *(strokes his cheek)*
Come on. I bet you say that to all the girls.

ALCESTE
How can you joke about it? The world

68

you inhabit turns betrayal into a game –
only there are no rules, and no sense of shame.
You've just amused yourself with me
(of course, I instinctively
knew that, and everything she's said
confirms things I already
suspected). But I had no real conception
that such effortless deception
was innate.
I warn you: you've chosen the wrong person to
    humiliate.
I accept that you have every right
to love who you like, to spend the night
with who you like. Love – clearly – can't be forced
on someone any more than it can be divorced
from passion. Yes – I understand desire –
but not the chronic need to be a liar.
What was it you said to me?
'Love is a word I don't use lightly'?
If that's the case
then not just love but life itself is meaningless:
and we reach the terminal stage
where there's no feeling left – only rage.
I feel physically sick
just at the thought of it.
You have no soul.
(I think I'd better leave before I lose control.)

JENNIFER

Leave? You can't make serious (I assume) accusations
then just walk out of the situation.

ALCESTE

Really? I should've walked out of this
the moment I became suspicious
instead of falling even more in love
and being made a complete fool of.

JENNIFER

You're intriguing me. I'm completely unaware
of what I've done.

ALCESTE

How can you stand there
and deny the truth
when I have proof?

*He produces a mobile and switches it to speakerphone.
We hear a message left by Jennifer. In contrast to her
usual style, she sounds hesitant and vulnerable.*

JENNIFER'S VOICE (*breath*)

It's me. Are you there? (*Breath.*) Look,
I really need to talk. (*Breath.*) I feel very alone here
and you're my only friend. (*Breath.*) I just wanted to
hear your voice. Sorry. OK. Call me.

Alceste switches off the phone. Slight pause.

JENNIFER

How did you get that? You have / no right to –

ALCESTE (*faint laugh*)

Look at you. You've gone completely white.

JENNIFER

How did you access that? Have you been tapping my
phone?

ALCESTE (*mocking*)

'My only friend', 'I feel so alone'.

JENNIFER

Have you?

ALCESTE

You admit it's your voice.

JENNIFER

Yes. Of course. Do I have any *choice*?

ALCESTE

You admit you're having a relationship
with this man – not just a friendship.

JENNIFER

Yes. No. What man? You're going too fast for me.

ALCESTE

Come on, come on: are you asking me
to believe this loving tone
isn't exclusively reserved for our friend Covington?

JENNIFER

Covington? (*Faint laugh.*) I totally fail to understand.

ALCESTE

My source is impeccable. *And*
it took a great deal of persuasion
believe you me to obtain this information.

JENNIFER

Wait a minute.

Slight pause.

I realise you've somehow gotten this from Marcia . . .
But isn't it obvious the message is for her?

ALCESTE

Oh absolutely. Yes. Obvious.
Please accept my humble apologies.
How dare you insult my intelligence
by twisting the evidence!
Why would you ever be so vulnerable and intimate
with a woman you're widely known to hate?
Well? Shall we listen to it again
while you / attempt to –

JENNIFER

                    I could never explain

anything to you. How dare you assume you have the authority
to invade my privacy?

Alright, alright.
Calm down. Let's see you try and shed a favourable
light / on this.

You don't own me. It doesn't matter
to me *what* you think. (Don't flatter / yourself.)

OK. I'm sorry. Look; just say
what would make you talk to Marcia that way.

(*coldly and calmly*)
No. It's for Covington.
I've fallen head over heels in love with him.
You're right: he's well-bred
well-read
exquisite (how did you guess?) in bed.
In fact I agree with everything you've said.
Just leave me alone – alright –
then I can get on with fucking every man in sight.

Alceste slaps her face.

You know something: you're completely mad.
I've just lost any respect I ever had
for you. Your assumption of betrayal
is so predictably male
and your resort to violence
speaks volumes. No. Please. Silence
is infinitely preferable to hearing
    how ashamed et cetera et cetera
you now are.
Y'know, what's so endearing

72

is for me to realise
you've assumed from day one I've been telling lies:
my most intimate confession
of love has been treated throughout with paranoia
  and suspicion.
I tell you I'm in love with you
but, oh no, nothing's ever good enough for you
(and you wonder why I feel isolated and alone
and leave pathetic messages on that woman's phone).
I'm angry.
And I have every right to be.
I naively make a commitment
and in return this is the treatment
I get. (*Bitterly.*) They say what I'm doing is
  pornography –
so why don't I stimulate that jealousy
of yours. Yes – why don't I see whether
I can't call some nice young boy right now so you can
  watch us making out together.

ALCESTE

There's nothing remotely naïve
about you. D'you really expect me to believe
this victim acting? Don't you see:
you are my destiny.
I shan't let go:
however low you sink I'm going to follow.

JENNIFER

That's not love, it's a psychiatric *disorder.*

ALCESTE

Maybe, maybe it borders
on it, yes. Sometimes I think the whole idea
of love is mad. The fear
of betrayal, of rejection – the reckless pursuit
of one's own personal humiliation. But the root
goes too deep.

73

I wish there was a way of keeping
you entirely to myself. Imagine if you were blind,
say, or paralysed. You'd find
out how loyal I was, because then
there'd be no other men
sniffing around. I'm the only one you see who wouldn't
   hurt you
or immediately desert you.
I'd have no rival
and you'd depend on me – literally – for your survival.
Where're you going?

                JENNIFER
           You're frightening me.
What kind of weird fantasy
is that?

              ALCESTE
   Jennifer.

              JENNIFER
       No.
Will you please let go
of me.

He lets go. Pause.

       You've had too much to drink.
OK?

She backs away.

So please: just leave me alone and give me time to think.

She turns suddenly and goes into her bedroom.
Alceste swallows the remainder of his drink.

Act Five

Darkness.

A figure appears carrying a lighted candelabrum. He's dressed as a servant at the court of Louis XIV. He moves round the room and lights more candles.

As the light grows we see that the hotel room has been transformed – by hangings and ornaments – into the baroque. There is an open harpsichord with an erotic painting inside the lid.

As the servant figure – Simon – moves downstage he finds Alceste slumped asleep in a chair. Simon shakes him gently.

SIMON

Monsieur? Monsieur?

Alceste wakes up.

ALCESTE
What the fuck . . .?

SIMON *(mysteriously)*
Voici bien des mystères.

Pause.

ALCESTE

Who are you?

SIMON
Nous sommes mal, Monsieur, dans nos affaires.

ALCESTE
I don't speak French. Why are you dressed
like that? I'm sorry but I'm not impressed.

SIMON

Monsieur, il faut faire retraite.

ALCESTE

What?

SIMON

Il faut d'ici déloger sans trompette.

ALCESTE

Speak to me in / English.

SIMON

Il faut partir, Monsieur, sans / dire adieu.

ALCESTE

Speak to me in English will you
or I'll fucking kill you.

*He grabs Simon, but after a moment relaxes his grip.
Simon disdainfully disengages himself and continues
with his preparations of the room.*

I'm sorry. Look I'm sorry I spoke
to you like that.

He looks round the room.

What is this then? Some kind of practical joke?

*John appears, laughing softly. He too is dressed in an
elaborate seventeenth-century costume – and all
subsequent entries will be in costumes in the
extravagant style of Louis' court – the men rivalling the
women. Only Alceste remains in his original clothes.*

JOHN

What's wrong? Have you forgotten about the party?

ALCESTE

Party? I was asleep –
or at least I was until that Gallic creep
woke me up. You're not really dressing up are you?

76

JOHN

I already have – and I've got something here for you.

He gives Alceste a box.

ALCESTE

What's this?

JOHN

Open it.

ALCESTE

D'you know I was dreaming
of wild animals. They were screaming
and biting into the most vulnerable places
imaginable. Then I saw they all had human faces.

Pause.

What is this?

JOHN

A wig.

ALCESTE (*faint laugh*)
No. I'm sorry.

JOHN

Come on. You're not going to let everybody
down? It would look bad.

ALCESTE

You must be mad
if you think I'm wearing this.

JOHN

It might be an improvement.

ALCESTE

Don't take the piss
out of me.

JOHN

I don't honestly see what harm a / wig can –

ALCESTE

I don't participate in costume fucking drama.

JOHN

Put it on.

ALCESTE

No.

John tries to put the wig on Alceste, who resists with increasing violence.

JOHN

Come on. You're so *uptight.*

ALCESTE

Just take it off. Take it off. I'm not having it. Alright?

He throws the wig down. Pause. John picks it up and smooths it.

JOHN

Was that strictly necessary? Wigs are expensive.
Listen, why / can't you –

ALCESTE

Yes. I know. I'm being childish and offensive
et cetera et cetera. Well let me reimburse you.
Nothing could be worse,
could it, than being in your debt.
Come on. How much? Cash or cheque?

He reaches for his money.

JOHN *(embarrassed)*

Please.

ALCESTE

Everything has a price,

and if my own particular vice
is to express my undying hatred
of human nature, then I'm quite prepared to pay for it.

JOHN

Come *on* . . .

ALCESTE

Come on *what*?
'Be reasonable'? That's about the only argument you've
    got.
Can you really tell me to my face
that you love the human race?
Or being in this artificial place?
That you don't dream of somewhere out in space
where this shallow world is not 'all that is the case'?

JOHN

No, no. Absolutely fine.
You don't need (obviously) to read Wittgenstein
to know that even by his or her own evaluation
man is an imperfect creation.
OK?
Our world is shallow. Accepted.
It doesn't follow that you have to reject it.
Surely its very superficiality
is what gives rise to interesting strategies
for survival. If there's no intrinsic meaning
then the fun is to invent one. This evening's
party is a perfect example.
How can you possibly perceive it as harmful?
I'm getting depressed by all your crises.
What good are all your so-called virtues if you can't
    enjoy their corresponding vices.

Offers the wig again.

Come on: do it for me.

ALCESTE

I've had enough for one day of your Mr Feel-Good
    philosophy.
Strategies? Meaning? Imperfection?
You have a wonderful gift for self-deception.
You claim academic innocence
while providing the rationale for decadence
of every kind. Every corrupt society enlists
its own tame apologists
and you're turning into one of them:
the kind of person
who paints over a moral mess
with borrowed intellectual fancy-dress.

JOHN

(Please, please, please . . .)

ALCESTE

Look at you. It's embarrassing.

JOHN (*shrugs*)
                              Embarrassing? It's fun.

ALCESTE

No. I'm sorry. Not everyone
would agree that what went on at Versailles
was 'fun'. Just try
imagining a church and state
monitoring every move you make:
what you write, what you think, who you meet . . .

JOHN

OK, OK. You're still drunk. Why don't you just go
    back to sleep?

ALCESTE

I'm quite sober.
And I tell you: when this party's over
I'm going. And I'm taking Jennifer

out of this. I'm just waiting for
the right moment to tell her. In the morning this will
    just seem

JOHN
I know, I know: like a bad dream.
Fine. Well look, I promised I'd meet Ellen at the desk.

He heads towards the door.

ALCESTE
OK. You know, I'm not depressed
about this. She's going to agree.
I know that secretly she has great respect for me.

JOHN
Absolutely. Well there's no telling
what will happen. I must go down and see Ellen.

John goes out.

*A moment passes. We hear voices and laughter.
Jennifer and Covington emerge from the bedroom, both
in beautiful costumes, Jennifer holding Covington's
script from Act One. They are not aware of Alceste
concealed in the chair downstage.*

COVINGTON
I wrote the part specifically for you.
You know how much I adore
your work.

JENNIFER
    Well, thank you.

COVINGTON
            And perhaps if you could use your
influence and show this to a producer . . .?
It's conceived for the stage but could be
very easily developed into a full-scale movie.

81

Pause. He looks at her.

JENNIFER

What is it?

COVINGTON (*lowers voice*)
Alceste. Can I be very personal
and ask if the two of you . . .? It's just there are some awful
rumours going round and I wondered if there was any truth in it.
(By the way: he's not to know you've got this script.)

JENNIFER (*faint laugh*)
Are you hitting on me?
I don't understand. And why the need for secrecy?

COVINGTON
Certain things are best
left unexplained. But it's no secret that I detest
him. (*He takes her hand.*) And the fact is –
yes – I find you extremely extremely attractive.

ALCESTE (*reveals himself*)
I'm *sure* you do. And it's obviously mutual
judging from the way you're blushing like a schoolgirl.
You talk about commitment and you let him
into your *bed*room
to what? Discuss his play?
Come on. I wasn't born yesterday.

COVINGTON
Can we please deal with this rationally.
I have no intention of trespassing on your territory.

ALCESTE
And I have no intention of waiting
here watching you salivating.

COVINGTON
She obviously prefers Neanderthals.

ALCESTE
No no. She clearly prefers the company of fools.

COVINGTON (*goes to Jennifer*)
I won't make a scene. He's obviously frightened.

ALCESTE
You? Make a scene? You can't even *write* one.

COVINGTON (*to Jennifer*)
I really think you ought to intervene.

ALCESTE (*to Jennifer*)
I think it's time you told us what / all this *means.*

COVINGTON
Isn't there some way of / *pacifying* him?

ALCESTE
Refusing to speak isn't going to satisfy anyone.

COVINGTON
You're not really in love with this paralytic?

ALCESTE
You're not really sleeping – are you – with a critic?

JENNIFER
Boys, boys. It must be time for your medication.
I feel like I'm in an institution watching the patients.
D'you really think I'm such a child
that I can't make up my own mind?
D'you both respect me so little
that resolving your own quarrel
is more important than considering my feelings?
Quite frankly nothing could be less appealing
to me than your undisguised

jealousy. And someone's going to be unpleasantly
    surprised
when they *do* see
the real me.
If you were even remotely sensitive –
either of you – you'd know that I'm being tentative
only because I find you both rather scary.

To Alceste.

And what's wrong with you? You haven't said a word
    about what I'm wearing.

COVINGTON
Then let me apologise. But even so
you can't equivocate.

ALCESTE
                    And I have a *right* to know.
Just what *is* the truth?
What *is* the 'real you'?
The dress,
yes,
is very beautiful . . .

JENNIFER
Thank you.

ALCESTE
. . . but entirely – and stunningly – superficial.
If this . . . man really is your lover
then obviously our relationship is over.
I apologise for my previous (yes, I'm sorry) violence
but please see that you no longer have a right to silence.

COVINGTON
Absolutely. Prevaricating
like this is simply self-incriminating.

84

JENNIFER

Oh, is that a fact?

What is this? Some kind of British neo-fascist double-
act?

I've told you: you'll both just have to keep waiting.

Ellen! My *God*! You look totally *devastating*!

*Ellen has appeared in costume, accompanied by John.
Laughing, she kisses cheeks with Jennifer.*

I'm so pleased to see you. I had visions
of being burned by the Inquisition
here. These two charming creatures
are worse than the Society of fucking Jesus.
Thank God I have an ally.
Look at them: can't you see they're just dying
to get the thumbscrews out.

ELLEN (*tries to take her aside*)

Listen, there's something we need to talk about.

JENNIFER (*laughing*)

Seriously. I was scared.

ELLEN (*as before*)

No. Listen. I think you need to be prepared / for this.

COVINGTON

Is there something we're not supposed to hear?

JENNIFER

Can't you just fuck off for a moment. Go on. /
Disappear.

ALCESTE

Don't talk to him like that. You've no right / to be
abusive.

JENNIFER

No right? Since when did you acquire this interest in
what is or is not polite?

85

Give me some space, OK? I just want
to speak privately to my . . . whatever you are.

ELLEN

Confidante.

JENNIFER

Confidante. Exactly.

Before they can speak, Julian, Alex and Marcia – all
costumed – enter brusquely, carrying bundles of the
evening paper, which they dump on the floor.

JULIAN

Well, well, well. They do indeed exist:
the mythical female icon and the uncompromising
  journalist.

ALEX (*coldly*)

Jenny darling, what a wonderful dress.
And Ellen – let's all drink shall we to the freedom of
  the gutter press.

Alex and Simon hand out champagne over the
following.

ELLEN

(I tried to / warn you.)

MARCIA

Yes, yes, yes. I know you can't stand the sight of me
but remember darling, you did invite me.
I was just gluing on my beauty spot
when – my God – I got
the most amazing phone call from Alex
asking me if I'd seen the evening paper. Of course
  we all know how he panics –
don't you Alex – so of course I read the piece
expecting it to be just sleaze,
the usual nasty prying journalese.

86

But unless you've been seriously misquoted
then even someone like myself . . . a devoted
friend . . . I mean I'm all for speaking one's mind,
but . . .

JULIAN
I think you're being far too kind,
Marcia. The whole thing quite frankly stinks.

ALEX
I mean if this is really what she thinks / of us . . .

JULIAN
I don't know which is more demeaning:
saying it or printing it. Yes, we've all been
hurt sometimes by the papers – but never attacked
like this. Let me read a typical extract:
'It's amazing to be sitting just feet away from a young
    woman whose controversial screen performances
    have divided the critics and become iconic for the
    click-and-consume YouTube generation.'
Blah blah blah.
'My first question is about Julian St John Smith,
    whose frequent admissions to private clinic The
    Priory are said to outnumber' –
that is a lie –
'his on-screen appearances. When I ask what she
    thinks of him, she is surprisingly frank.'
and I quote
"Poor Julian is a kind of caricature of all the bad
    things you hear about the British – class-obsessed,
    vain and emotionally retarded. He's also a terrible
    actor."'
Unquote.

JENNIFER
Ellen, this was *not part* of the interview.

JULIAN

Excuse me. May I continue?

'I ask her what it's like to meet Covington, a critic who
   has consistently championed her work on this side of
   the Atlantic. She gives a sphinx-like smile and says:'
quote
'I was fascinated. The man's an awesome combination
   of arrogance and intellectual emptiness. It's true
   he's written favourably about me in the past, but
   the sad fact is dead white male critics have a
   tendency to admire any young woman who takes
   her clothes off in front of the camera.'

JENNIFER

I don't understand. You've abused our friendship.

MARCIA

You should be more careful who you get into bed with.

ALEX (*takes over reading*)

'Over vodka martinis on the roof garden with its
   stunning panorama of the river the conversation
   turns to top actors' agent Alexander Alvi. Is it true,
   I ask, that without Alex she'd never have made the
   transition to major star status? Her response is
   refreshingly blunt: "Alex's input into my career has
   been less than zero. He has his own reasons for
   cultivating me – well two reasons to be precise –
   greed and lust." I ask I her finally . . .'

JENNIFER

Alex . . .

Slight pause.

ALEX

'I ask her finally to comment on her much-rumoured
   relationship with writer Alceste. Is he, I suggest,
   a kind of father-figure to her? She stares for a while

into her glass before gazing up at me with those
mysterious brown eyes. "I can't think of anyone,"
she says, "less like my father, who is gentle, quiet,
respected and respectful of others. Alceste thinks of
himself as a kind of misanthrope, but I sometimes
suspect that deep down he's maybe just one more
good old-fashioned misogynist."
Her outspoken self-confidence makes it hard to believe
that this beautiful young woman has only just
emerged from her teens . . .'
Et cetera et cetera.

He lets the paper fall. Silence.

JENNIFER
I thought we were friends, Ellen. I invited you here as
a *guest*.

ELLEN
I have my career to think of – and I do believe this is
in the public interest.

ALEX
Well Jenny, you are a real model of loyalty –
what wonderful news for the whole agency –
because whatever you may feel about my – what was
it? – 'greed', did she write, and 'lust'
you are my client and as such we have a bond of trust.
And to say it's about the money is such total bollocks:
your whole career's worth less than just ONE –
sweetheart – of my Jackson Pollocks.
(We're going to need more than lawyers to handle
this kind of scandal.)

JULIAN
Great article. *Loved* the style.
No, I really don't think it's worth my while
getting angry. Who cares about you and your dykey
friend when I can have any woman I bloody well like.

COVINGTON

And what about my script?
She promised me she'd commit to it!
She's obviously made so many promises
they've become meaningless.
Well, I've behaved like a complete idiot
haven't I? But at least you've made me realise it
in time. I'm sure you'll always be in the news,
Jenny. Just don't expect any more good reviews.

To Alceste.

I apologise for what happened earlier on today.
Obviously I have no intention of standing in your way.

MARCIA

I came here as you can imagine fully intending
to take your side – desperately wanting to defend
you – but you are clearly, my darling, morally deformed.
And I have to say to everyone: you *were* warned.
(And how anyone could write this kind of feature
with no reference whatsoever to Jenny's most
    significant teacher . . .)
But the person who must be the most cut up
and hurt is this poor man / whose integrity –

ALCESTE

                                            Just shut up
will you for once. You're not my wife,
and you can kindly keep your nose out of my
    emotional life.
Don't think I don't know the price
you're asking for taking my side in this –
a considerable amount
(and I don't think I could bring myself to settle the
    account).

MARCIA

Don't flatter yourself. *Wife?* What makes you think
    I'd want to be
sold into paternalistic slavery
with you? Marriage is just an anachronism
darling – a relic of late-twentieth-century capitalism
or didn't you know? And I think I'd be afraid to get
    my kicks
from Jennifer's rejects.
(After all I'm not someone who happily caters
for people of dubious immunological status.)
I have no wish to 'come between you' whatsoever
and I'm sure you'll be terribly terribly terribly happy
    together.

ALCESTE

So. You've all had your little say
then, just like in an old play
where everyone makes a speech.

Pause.

And now it's my turn,
only for once / I . . .

JENNIFER

OK, OK everyone, burn
me then, at the stake. You're after
blood – clearly – and hey! I'm the martyr.
Mistakes have been made – yes –
and I can see that this is where I'm expected to confess
et cetera et cetera and beg forgiveness.
But as God is my witness
I'm no more guilty of deception
than any other person standing in this room –
with perhaps one notable exception.

To Alceste.

You're the only one here who doesn't take me
for granted. And you have every right to hate me.
I'm sorry.

ALCESTE
D'you think I'm so disloyal
as to judge you by a sound-bite in a newspaper article?
It's obvious to me you've been provoked
into making these comments. (*To Ellen.*) And I'd've
    hoped
that for all your intellectual wheeler-dealing
you might have spared some thought for this girl's
    feelings.
How you can vandalise
a person's soul in search of scandal is
beyond me. Fortunately the truth of human
nature can't be condensed into your squalid little
    column.

To Jennifer.

Listen: we have so much in common:
we're quick to be judgemental
and both unfashionably sentimental
and this is what I propose:
no more films, acting, parties, interviews.
Quit the city. Forget work. Turn our backs
on all of this. Begin to relax.
Just the two of us.
We can become anonymous.
We'll buy a little house
with a garden – trees – a stream – whatever.
Then we could think about starting – don't you see –
    a / family together.

JENNIFER (*crescendo of disbelief*)
No, no, no, no, no, no, no . . . *What? Leave?*
What're you trying to *do* to me? This is the air I breathe.

ALCESTE

We don't *need* these people. This hotel,
these costumes – it's like an ante-room to hell.
Look at them, Jennifer. *They* don't care.

JENNIFER (*faint laugh*)

You're seriously asking me to join you in some kind of
    suburban nightmare?
Shop? Cook? Clean? What? Do the dishes? *Sleep?*
Drive the kids to ballet in a Japanese *jeep?*

Ellen laughs softly.

'These people' are still (I hope) my friends – *and* –
like it or not – this is the world I understand.

*She takes Ellen's arm. The others grin, now they see
the tide is turning against Alceste.*

Maybe right now they're temporarily
a little mad at me –
but I know they'll soon enough forgive me.
Won't you Alex?

ALEX

Never.

JENNIFER (*offering her hand*)
Alex . . .

ALEX

Never.

JENNIFER
Alex, please . . .

ALEX

Never never never Jenny

yes of course I do.

He kisses her hand. They both laugh.

93

JENNIFER
Don't you see?
And Julian – poor baby – are you quite sure
that when you're kicked by me and whipped by me
    you don't come crawling back to me for more? –
mmm? – don't you deep down just love a girl who feeds
those dog-like sado-masochistic needs?

*Jennifer and Julian are also reconciled. Everyone
except Alceste laughs. Jennifer turns to him.*

It might've been fun for us to have an affair,
but I'll live how I like – and I'm not going anywhere.

The others all laugh softly.

(*Intensely.*) I love the city – and the night.
And no way will I abandon them without a fight.
Simon.

SIMON
Madame?

JENNIFER
                He makes such a wonderful
servant and his French is impeccable.
Let's have some music. And nothing too arty.
I'm sick of this. I want to party.

*The others laugh. Simon begins to play boogie-woogie
on the harpsichord, but after a moment Alceste makes
a violent gesture – bangs down the lid, or smashes a
plaster Cupid – and the music stops.*

ALCESTE
If that's the life you want to lead,
so be it. Just don't come to me when you need
help, because I shan't be there.
You may not believe in despair

but I do. It's a kind of pit
and you're digging yourself deeper and deeper into it.

He walks out. Embarrassed laughter.

JOHN

It's so typical of him to overreact.
Don't worry: I'll run and bring him straight back.

*John moves towards the exit but, at an imperceptible
gesture from Jennifer, Simon and Alex block his way.*

What're you doing? Look: I want to leave.
I'm worried about him.

ELLEN

Relax, John, just relax. Don't you see
we're better off without him.